As you try your wings
in this journey of your
life - we hope you will
remember us as we pray
for you.

*This book*
*is presented to*

*Linda*

*by*

*Amy. Sam Ciampa*

For the Graduate

Roots
&
Wings

James W. Angell

Abingdon Press

Nashville

# ROOTS AND WINGS

## Library of Congress Cataloging in Publication Data

ANGELL, JAMES W., 1920–
  Roots and wings.
    1. Youth—Conduct of life.  2. Youth—Religious
life.  I. Title.
BJ1661.A5      1983      248.8'3      83-2564

### ISBN 0-687-36585-6

Material on page 58 is from *Time for All Things* by Charlie
Shedd. Copyright © 1962 by Abingdon Press. Published
as a Festival Book by Abingdon Press, 1980. Used by
permission.

MANUFACTURED BY THE PARTHENON PRESS AT
NASHVILLE, TENNESSEE, UNITED STATES OF AMERICA

*A Salute to All Graduates*

# Contents

# Foreword

Here, at last, are some things which need to be said above the ambient noises of secular inducements to yield to the lowest common denominator of life. These things need to be said to our youngsters at this crucial time in their lives when life commitments are being looked at with a questioning hopefulness. In this book they will find needed enthusiastic encouragement.

Michael Novak would find joy in knowing that Dr. Angell shares the concern he expresses in "The Experience of Nothingness":

. . . The young have a right to learn a way of discriminating right from wrong, the posed from the authentic, the excellent from the mediocre, the brilliant from the philistine, the shoddy from the workmanlike. When no one with experience bothers to insist—to insist—on such discrimination, they rightly get the idea that discernment is not important, that no one cares, that no one cares either about such things—or about them. For it is demanding to teach children ethics, beauty, excellence; demanding in itself, and even more demanding to do with authenticity. . . .

The genius of communicating with compelling simplicity is a gift. James Angell says beautifully those things for which we all wish we could find the words to attract and interest our youngsters.

Clarence G. Scholl

# Preface

Among all the rites of passage it is hard to think of any more crowded with family significance and crazy ecstasy than high school graduation. It is the end of childhood, the launching pad of careers. It is celebration, mourning, birth, and death, all rolled up into a few days.

In *Roots and Wings* I have tried to commemorate what this unique life event is all about and to create a souvenir of love that parents, friends, churches, or other admirers might want to present to new graduates along with their own autographed good wishes.

It is not a How-to book, and I hope it isn't preachy. It is meant, instead, to sing a little, soar a little. To put these rare, marker moments in perspective.

I remember the night of my commencement. I was happy as could be. Still I wanted to find a secret corner where I could go off and unload a few tears, and I did. Then some of us went out for hamburgers, drove around the deserted county fairgrounds at the edge of town and let out a few yells.

Since then, I've attended four high school graduations for my own children. Each of these, too, has become a night to remember and to delight in.

Today's graduates are impressively mature, and perhaps some of what I have written and collected won't sound as adult as it should.

Still, I insist that high school graduation is and always will be a special rendezvous with idealism, a first fling at naming a life direction, and a time of appreciation for the gifts of roots and wings.

James W. Angell

**roots** : The usually underground portion of a plant that serves as support, draws food and water from the surrounding soil.

**wings** : A means of rapid ascent.

—from the *American Heritage Dictionary*

# Graduation Daze

*Snug-fitting, square-topped caps with dangling tassels. Beautiful presents, a few tears. Printed announcements. Parties and processional practice under morning sunlight at the athletic field.*

*Mellow, mysterious feelings. The exchanging of kisses. Yearbook autographs. Skip day. Turning in the old band uniform. The last time, I guess, I'll ever walk through this door . . .*

*Mother. Dad. Younger brother. Older sister. Picture-taking in the backyard. A diploma.*

*Now it's over.*

*I'm an alum.*

If you're soon to be graduated from high school, if that wonderful, woozy experience is waiting for you down the road a few months or days hence, this book is for you.

It talks about the challenge of ongoing growth and life excitement as you move from one dimension of experience into another—as you revel in the flair of these adolescent years and at the same time master the skill of bidding them good-bye.

A high school girl graduate, full of appreciation for her set of years that was ending, and aware she would soon be leaving home, wrote a letter to her parents in which she summed up the legacy she felt they had given her.

"You gave me the two most precious things any parents can ever give their children," she wrote. "You gave me roots and wings."

If you can't honestly say those gifts have come to you by way of adoring, interested parents, perhaps some day you'll have the opportunity to give them to others . . . to your own kids.

*. . . with dangling tassels*

## Mom and Dad—You Gave Me

You gave me roots and wings.

Birth. A welcome to greet my opening eyes and life. A smile. A name. A home.

Dry pants, food, and peek-a-boo. Shoulders to be burped on. Knees to be bounced upon. Touchings. A strong handgrip as we crossed the street.

Rides on the merry-go-round and ferris wheel. Cello lessons. A chance to borrow the family car—"we'll leave the lights on."

Laughter at the supper table.

A sense of how important it is to tell the truth, not to be lazy. Prayer as privilege more than duty.

Apple-blossom beauty without. Good-feelings beauty within. Praise. Lots of praise. Songs to sing. Winter coats and birthday cakes. Answers to my questions. Confessions of your ignorance when you didn't know.

A listening heart. The right to some mistakes.

Help with math. An allowance. Trips we took. Troubles we shared. Things we said to each other in the dark. The prom formal, the football team.

Thermometers and medicines. Dreams, patches, telephone calls, and camp. Kisses on the top of my head. Patience with my angers. Rebuke for my conceit.

So much to remember. So much to believe in, hope for.

Not only roots and wings.

You gave me time. Love. Yourself. Dignity. God.

An awareness of my own history, a vision of someone to become.

# The Imperishables

Some imperishables I have and cling to:

Roots that reach down into my subterranean self, like the invisible, ground-clutching fingers of a tall redwood tree, and a dawning sense of what is permanent in the universe.

Confidence that I am radically, personally loved by God, not as a term of theology but as a friend. Faith, not as a clump of unchanging doctrinal certainties, but as an active, day-by-day relationship with God.

Belief in my own irreplaceable, unrepeatable life as something significant. Important to God. To the cosmos.

Trust that God is with me wherever I go. Psalm 139 says it best. God in my joys. In my panicked moments, too.

Plus the belief that life is too precious to be spent mainly in self-indulgence, which is what our culture at times seems to recommend.

That my failures are never final.

That there is no real life for myself unless I can discover a way also to affirm the needs and rights of others. Justice and freedom for the few will not do.

Belief—meaning faith, confidence, trust.

# Benefits of Remembering

$A$ best seller in the second half of the seventies was Alex Haley's *Roots*—the story of his heritage as a black man. He found that his great-great-great-great grandfather came to America from Africa on September 29, 1767, as part of a cargo of ninety-eight slaves, transported on the *H.M.S. Lord Ligonier*.

Two hundred years later to the day, Haley went down to the wharf at Annapolis, Maryland, where the *Ligonier* had unloaded. There he rendezvoused with the memory of the arriving of his forebear, Kunta Kinte. Haley's five-generation story became a national phenomenon and sent thousands of other people into strongboxes and library stacks to reclaim their heritage.

As you start down the aisle, probably to the accompaniment of "Pomp and Circumstance," you, too, will be remembering: your home and own bedroom, your brothers and sisters; maybe a touchdown you made, or the night you and your friends draped the trees on the school ground with toilet tissue; bright moments and some bad moments, grade reports and grade school. All these "memory tapes" are filed away for future reference, and most of them will wind up blessing you and mellowing your tomorrow.

When we remember and notice what God has done, that's called worship. It's realizing after some consideration that whatever happens in our lives—our mistakes, victories, conflicts, and conquests—can be woven or rewoven into the pattern of a purpose.

Looking back can sometimes turn us into pillars of salt. Nostalgia is a wistful or excessively sentimental yearning for return to some period, condition, or setting in the past. Still, looking back is part of the process of finding out who we are, and there is profit in that.

James Thurber gives good advice: Do not look back in regret, nor forward in fear, but around you in awareness.

# Not What You Are Going to Be—Who

Dr. William Glasser wrote a book entitled *The Identity Society*. In this book he says that one of the things that has happened in the lifetime of most of us is a shift from *goal*-oriented to *role*-oriented living.

"*What* are you going to be?" How often have you been asked that? Are you going to be a businessman? An engineer? A doctor? A teacher? Goals seem necessary, logical.

Dr. Glasser says the question that overtook that one, though, around 1950, was not *what* but *who* are you going to be? To be tabbed a pharmacist, professional athlete, artist, scientist, mechanic, or mortician was not, we came to understand, the most important thing to be said about any human being. It wasn't and isn't the most important thing we have to decide. We are more than a bundle of skills. Life is more than a job.

After Gerald Ford was defeated for the presidency in 1976 and was returned by the voters to private citizenship, a political editor wrote of him, "He's about to discover what we may all discover if we live long enough . . . exactly who we are without a job classification . . . whether that be full-time mother, president, stockbroker, or lieutenant. He may help us think about how much of our ego depends upon the things we may eventually lose."

Though we revere those who have gone ahead of us, chopping out a path through the rain forests of the unknown, we are not our ancestors any more than we are our vocations. We are not *where* we live, nor the color of our skin. We are not, in the center of ourselves, Republicans, Yankees, Southerners, or Methodists, grandparents, or husbands or wives; we are the children of God—each as unique as a January snowflake.

To some extent, the answer to the question, Who am I? is constantly changing. One day we answer it by saying: I am a child in the third grade at Condit School. The next by saying: a sophomore at Ohio State. The day after that: I'm retired now, I used to teach law.

I am a mother of two. A Jew. Executive with Alcoa. Captain, Eastern Air Lines. Secretary working on the tenth floor. Prime Minister. Patient. Chinese. Blind. Atheist. Social Security Number. West Pointer. Son of Flying Cloud. Debutante. Divorcée. Ph.D. Amputee. Sailor. Saint. Florist. Prisoner 552160. A newborn babe.

We are many people in one, but when the layers of transiency are stripped away, there is also something wonderful and indestructible beneath this cultural veneer. I am *a part of a plan.*

# What Will College Be Like?

*(A game of adjectives. Make your own four best guesses.)*

**Scary . . . Wonderful . . . Friendly
Lonely . . . Hard . . . Adult
Experimental . . . Sleepless . . . Exhilarating
New . . . Noisy . . . Neat . . . Independent
Beautiful . . . Expensive . . . Fun
Bookish . . . Dressy . . . Mysterious
Relaxed . . . Interesting . . . Fattening
Entertaining . . . Profitable
Soul-Stretching . . . Maturing . . . Happy
Unsettling . . . Fascinating . . . Unforgettable
Confusing . . . Perfect
—All of the above—**

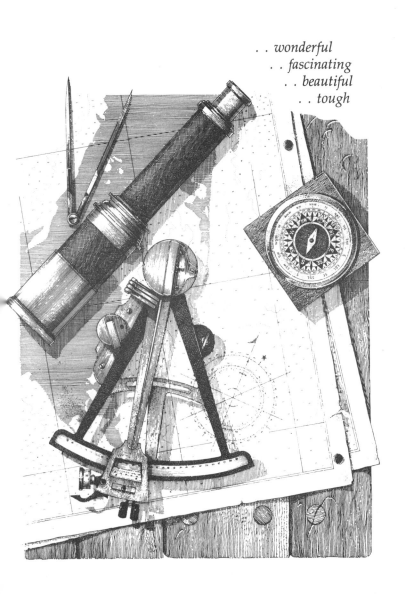

*. . wonderful*
*. . fascinating*
*. . beautiful*
*. . tough*

Not everyone can sing.

But everyone, with no exceptions, has a heart capable of making music. Find something in the world that will do that to you and for you.

Will it be research? A career in the theater? Space technology? Raising children of your own? Flowers? Friendship? Peace Corps service in another country?

Choose those things that make you happy. Life is a party to be celebrated more than a problem to be solved.

# We Are What We Choose

Every day we come up against a choice where our identity or a lack of identity is on the line.

Three teen-age boys from a small town in Texas were stopped by police. They were driving a big, expensive automobile, and a police investigation revealed that the boys were carrying $500,000 in cash. They had been on a spree and had spread other thousands of dollars around record shops, motels, and clothing and jewelry stores.

The same day the story appeared, another on the same page told how a certain hospital had just acquired a sonic scanner that increased their capacity to diagnose and treat diseases in some new ways. It cost the same amount—$500,000.

One of the answers to the identity question is: We are what we *choose*.

Sometimes we choose wrong.

One Christmas a Christian high school student printed a copy of a carol and underlined or circled the name of Jesus at each place in the song. Then, with an air of superiority, thrust it into the face of a Jewish classmate. Another student who witnessed this exchange later told her mother, "—— is so busy being religious, she's forgotten what religion means."

What does God require of me?

To be kind.

This doesn't take those of us off the hook who do nothing or say nothing about the faith we follow, who leave all such conversations to others.

We may hesitate about discussing our personal faith with others on the grounds of privacy, not wanting to butt into someone else's life uninvited. But if we genuinely care about others, some sharing of what has become important to us is inevitable and right.

*I'm sorry—but if it were a perfect world there would be nothing for us to do.*

*—Letter from a friend following a personal tragedy*

To have no more physical dangers to brave, no more intellectual questions to answer, no more moral and ethical and spiritual peaks to climb—that is the most barren plight of all. For a "man's reach does exceed his grasp," and that is what a heaven is for. It is a place in which we reject any whimpering wish to crawl back into that static state of tranquil irresponsibility and instead march gladly forth into this vale of soul-making, affirming this old world of ours as:

a hazardous place in which to be safe, but
a glorious place in which to be brave;
a confusing place in which to be sure, but
a fascinating place in which to be curious;
a devil of a place in which to harvest a soul, but
God's own kind of place in which to grow one.

—Melvin Wheatley

"If goodness lead him not, yet weariness
May toss him to my breast."

—George Herbert, "The Pulley"

# My Country 'Tis of Thee—
## Or Politics and Me

Politics has a bad reputation.

Politics makes us think of cigar smoke and heavy deals, expensive campaign propaganda and winning at all costs.

But politics is also a noble science, and has been called "the art of the possible."

All progress in human society has to be negotiated. There have to be compromises and a testing of ideas or positions through debate, and anyone who participates in such processes is acting politically.

As you move out of the high school scene where you've already gained some political experience, seen power both used and misused—maybe even run for office yourself—it's not a bad idea to decide that you're going to keep on making politics part of your personal agenda, regardless of what vocation you settle upon or where you live.

A great English statesman, Edmund Burke, said many years ago that all that is needed for evil to gain the upper hand in human affairs is for decent people to do nothing. So those who wash their hands of politics are definitely not neutral; they have voted by their silence or reluctance to get involved.

Both freedom and the privilege of self-government are made of fragile materials, like peanut brittle, and we have no assurance that we can either gain these gifts or keep them indefinitely.

All in favor say aye.

## "He Woke Up My Life"

It was one of those informal therapy groups, but it wasn't being held in the conversation lounge of a psychiatric hospital. It was in a prison chapel, a low barracks-type building with beige asphalt tile on the floor. The windows that opened out onto the compound where other prisoners were playing softball looked like they hadn't been washed lately.

The fellow who was speaking was black and twenty-four years old. He was telling the others about the wrongdoing that had brought about his sentence. It was a Seven-Eleven store robbery. It hadn't been his idea. He didn't even need the money, but he found himself swept along in an 11 P.M. plot that seemed as if it were just another slice of police story television—something entered into more for excitement than for profit. But one of the fellows had carried a real gun, not just a toy pistol, and he realized now how serious that was.

He wasn't arguing that he had gotten a "bum rap." But he was saying that prison had brought him face-to-face with himself as never before and that, when the time for release came, he had important new uses in mind for his life.

Speaking of a friend who had helped him believe that there was still time left to make a new start, to use his mistakes as building blocks for his future rather than as a permanent condemnation, he said, "He woke up my life!"

Moments of awakening are part of self-emergence. Most of us won't have to wait for such troubles or problems to experience them. But they probably will come to us—lightning flashes in the darkness—and when they do we should grab hold and let them carry us upward, closer to the stars.

We learn by touching.

We love by touching.

We gain emotional poise by being touched. If there is distance, fear, or embarrassment in touching, we are without the freedom God means for us to enjoy.

Obviously, touching can also get us into difficulty. We can't touch fire without getting hurt. Insincere touching also hurts.

There's a story about deceptive touching in the Old Testament. Isaac was old and blind. He had made up his mind to give his blessing—the right to succeed as the head of the family—to Esau, his oldest son, whom he regarded as more honest and reliable than his brother. But Jacob dressed himself in his brother's clothing and used animal skins to cover his arms and convinced the old, blinded father that he was Esau. Through this trick he gained the blessing for himself. That the act was irreversible, even though the ruse became quickly known, suggests how serious the gesture was.

Most touching is full of rewards. We are more complete human beings when we have learned to feel at home with people and with all the magic surfaces of the world.

"O world, I cannot hold thee close enough!" sang Edna St. Vincent Millay.

Thomas said to his Lord: "Let me touch your side in order that I may believe."

Please touch.

Life is made for touching—and often reaches out to touch us. We make this remark, "What you said (or did) touched me deeply." This is a different way of touching, but still touching. People reach out and touch us with their eyes. They do selfless things to show love for us, and we feel their embrace in our core.

It may not be another person at all. Just the peacefulness of clouds, the beauty of bottle-brush, or the majesty of stars. We see something, hear something. It is life reaching out to touch us with one of its infinite benedictions.

## Growing by Hurting

It hurts!

You've said that already, more than once.

You fell and skinned your knee. The doctor gave you a shot. You had a sore throat.

Then there was a broken love affair, and you cried.

Somebody died, and that hurt.

Homesickness hurts.

Being betrayed or lied about hurts.

But hurting also introduces us to new latent strengths in ourselves. Our spiritual muscles develop fiber and power. And we start to buy into the human race—to begin to comprehend a world in which there is massive hurting and pleas for help.

Hurting is something that seems inevitable, that we try our best to avoid.

But hurting is also usually an opportunity. Sometimes, even a fantastic one.

## Blocked Doorways

"And when they could not get near [Jesus] because of the crowd, they removed the roof above him; and when they had made an opening, they let down the pallet on which the paralytic lay. And when Jesus saw their faith, he said to the man, 'My son, your sins are forgiven,'" (Mark 2:4, 5 RSV).

Jesus is in Capernaum on the far side of the sea called Galilee. Whether he is staying at Peter's house or has his own residence, isn't clear. Wherever he is, though, the news of his presence has spread and crowds have gathered so thickly about the front door there's no way to get inside.

The four who come carrying their handicapped friend are determined: they approach Jesus by way of a makeshift opening in the roof.

One night a girl and a guy arranged to meet another couple at a theater. They drove in separate cars, then met in a parking lot close-by so they could all attend the movie together. When it was over they returned to the parking lot to find themselves up against an old problem: keys for one of the cars were locked inside.

By luck a discarded coat hanger was discovered a few feet away (someone must have had the same trouble before), and, after twenty minutes of manipulating a makeshift wirehook thrust through a side window ("There now just a little more. Oh, you've just about got it!), the latch was tripped, and they were on their way to Louie's Yogurt Shop.

God often helps us find alternate roads to glory and to life.

Here's the doorway at Capernaum and it looks impassable. How about the roof?

We all have roofs that need to come off. Limits to what we think we can do which are, in fact, false.

Thomas Carlyle said: "Kites rise against the wind." And someone else has said that with God nothing is wasted.

Faith is both adoration and alternative. The doorway and the roof. Twisted coat hangers and a sad supper in an Upper Room that later turns into an Easter joy. All contribute, all help us, in one way or another, to learn to trust a love that will not let us go, that will not let us down, and that will not let us off.

# To Be a Person

I want to be me.
I mustn't be you.
You are wonderful.
You are successful.
You are nice, and
Have a pretty face.
But I cannot be you.
And (sorry if it hurts)
I don't want
To be you.

I want to dent
The face of life somewhere,
Somehow, with my
Own mark. Even if
I must be bad,
That's better than
Not being at all, or
Trying merely to be
Someone else.

I want to crawl out
Of the uterus of nothingness
Into someoneness. I
Want to sing my
Own song, die my
Own death. Let life
Know that I was here
And did my thing.

## Six Ways to Tell Right from Wrong

When you're in a situation in which you're not sure what to do, ask yourself some questions:

Is it true?

Will it stand public disclosure? Is it something I am willing for others to know about?

If I think of persons I admire the most, how do I imagine that they might feel about it? How might they decide or act in similar circumstances?

The Golden Rule (Matthew 7:12). Will it hurt someone?

Will it pass the test of friendship, of loyalty, of love?

Is it something I will someday be able to look back upon without regret?

## Forgiveness. Is That All?

He lies there on a padded board. And here's the Great Physician whose reputation is that he can make the blind see, the lame strong, the demonized sane.

The man wants so much to be healed. And his companions look into the face of the famous Jesus, asking: "Do you think you can help him?"

Jesus looks upon the supine, pathetic figure, then says quietly: "Your sins are forgiven."

There must have been an awful silence after that. A disappointment that screamed: "Is that *all* you can do for him? Is that *all?*"

The reaction must have been about the same as if someone were to come to you hungry, begging for something to eat, and you said, "I can't *give* you anything, but I'll sell you some insurance."

Or another came and said: "I'm cold. Will you give me something to wear to keep me warm?" And you replied: "I can't loan you a coat, but here's a book you might enjoy."

Or, as if a tired traveler said, "I'm lost. Can you help me find my way home?" And you said, "I can't help you find the way, but if you're ever in Los Angeles again, give me a call.''

Forgiveness?

Yes, because forgiveness opens the door to a relationship that is a higher gift, a stronger strength than a fast solution to a single, immediate problem.

If by forgiveness God's love and presence have come pouring into our lives, the rest can be managed.

Other needs can be faced and answers found.

If, on the other hand, we make God a warehouse, a problem-solver, need-satisfier, miracle worker, and skip his deeper meaning, one act of mercy, as Jesus knew, could mislead. Trust in God is for *all* of life's moments and hours and tests—not for only one or two.

We may have to go through the roof or around Robinhood's barn or switch to plan B. We may even find a way to be satisfied with less than our first desire. But a victory of faith is always possible.

## Make Peace with Yesterday

I'm glad that God takes every worn-out day and
  burns it up in sunset;
All mistakes, the little triumphs, and the futile cares
Are gathered into one bonfire that breaks in flame
  against the banks of sky.

I think He likes to see it burn and stand beside it till
  the last grey ashes fall.
And then across the fretful thoroughfares, over the
  troubled roofs and petty wars
Out of lonely heights of the unknown a clean wind
  blows all tangled up with stars.

—ANONYMOUS

There are two majorities, son, though you ask me
no question. The nameless dead, the unborn
legions of time. But we are the thin minority, the
living, who hold God's sceptre of light.

—A. M. Sullivan

## Grace Is the Bottom Line

Grace means that, having been given and having accepted forgiveness for our own mistakes, we also try to act charitably and non-judgmentally toward others.

It doesn't mean we abandon all distinctions.

It *does* mean we recognize the world isn't neatly divided into two groups—good people and bad people. We're all a little of both.

Virginia Satir seems to be referring to the gift of grace when she writes:

> I want to love you without clutching,
>     Appreciate you without judging,
>         Join you without invading,
>             Invite you without demanding . . .
> Leave you without guilt,
>     Criticize you without blaming,
>         And help you without insulting.
> If I can have the same from you,
> Then we can truly meet and enrich each other.

"Grace," says Lofton Hudson, "isn't just a blue-eyed blonde." It is gratitude, perspective, humility, the bottom line.

# The Will of God

Leslie Weatherhead was one of the great Christian thinkers of the modern era, and, for a number of years, he occupied the pulpit of City Temple, London. He also wrote several books.

He is much remembered for a small book in which he provides us helpful insight about what is meant by the phrase, "the will of God."

If something terrible happens—if thousands of people lose their lives in an earthquake or flood, is *that* the will of God? Is God able to prevent such disasters? If so, why are they not, in the name of justice and love, prevented? If not—if God is unable to stop them—who is finally in charge? These are big, big questions. And most of our answers to them are small and incomplete. Dr. Weatherhead's words help.

He divides the will of God into three parts. The *ultimate* will is what God intends for us: wholeness and happiness, life and joy. The *permissive* will is what God, in order to grant us freedom, has settled on—an imperfect world that is still being created, a more beautiful and exciting world than one in which we might have been fashioned as automatons with no great mountains left to climb, sacrifices to make, or hard things to endure. And in between lies the *circumstantial* will, where we may take what is, even the tough and painful things, and by faith transform them into victories of the spirit.

## I Believe in Myself

I believe in myself.

I believe there is a good kind as well as a bad kind of selfishness—that the right kind is a gift from God and a desirable personal goal.

I believe in my ability to make decisions and stay with them—even when others disagree with me and I am under pressure to change.

I believe in my own value to my family, friends, and society because I realize others are equally valuable to me.

I believe, not that I am above temptation, but that I am brave enough to admit the difference between right and wrong in most cases, and that I won't pretend that my choices are without moral consequence.

I believe in my ability to endure failure without concluding that it makes me a failure.

I believe in experiencing the freedom that comes from both receiving an apology and in saying I'm sorry for some of my own conduct.

I believe in my ability to endure hurt—including the thought of my own eventual dying—without a need to run from such truth.

I believe in myself because I believe that God believes in me. That gives meaning to my days and hope to my tomorrows.

## My Body

The New Testament tells us that our bodies are meant to be temples of God, not experimental vacuums for dangerous drugs, beer barrels, or trash containers (perpetual junk food).

Honor your body. Appreciate it as God's gift.

Care for it in a spirit of trusteeship. Enjoy the strength it contains.

Don't dissociate your sexual potential from your total potential to love, or from your summons to be a woman or man who is a credit to the race.

Take time to rest, to play, to exercise, to be alone. Learn the peace that comes from growing tired as the result of hard work.

Be interested in nutrition and whatever contributes to physical and mental alertness. Fast once in a while simply to remind yourself that you do not live exclusively by bread—or hamburgers.

Find the participant sport you like best and have a go at it, whether you show talent or not. Swim. Jog. Climb. Life isn't all party-time, but it is, indeed, a party.

One of the most discussed books of the generation that just preceded yours was George Orwell's *1984*. At the time it was written, it represented a frightening glimpse of the future.

That then-distant tomorrow is here.

It isn't all bad; but neither is it paradise come of age.

Let's start with the good.

—Today we live longer, healthier lives. We are better fed, housed, educated, and traveled. And we've discovered how much fun it is to exercise and keep the body in good shape.

—Today, more people reject racism, age-ism, and sexism than was true the year you were born. Then, a lot of us didn't know what those discussions were about, or even what questions to ask.

—Though many of our natural resources appear to be running out, the sense of crisis has brought a vastly accelerated awareness of the importance of being careful stewards of God's creation.

—Our country is now more clear-eyed about

its own faults and vulnerability than it was before the names of Vietnam and Kent State became branded into the hide of history.

But here is the discouraging news.

—The Nuclear Club is growing.
—The rich-poor chasm is widening—weekly.

People have found out, time and again, that money and ownership do not bring happiness. Many people are still miserable, even if they hold a Ph.D. and earn a six-figure income. The divorce rate is zooming. Crime rate, ditto. A hamburger might soon cost five dollars.

The kind of religion that says "It'll-get-you-what-you-want" has demonstrated more appeal than "It-may-ask-you-for-everything-you-have."

What this adds up to is that the eighties are, on balance, both a dangerous and a magnificent time in which to live. It is a period that is truer and tougher than the sixties and more dynamic and decisive than the seventies. But, most of all, it is filled with opportunities to show the splendor of the human spirit and the prize of excellence that awaits those who have the courage to endure.

# Six Loves

Arthur L. Mayer was an outstanding figure in the fields of exhibition, distribution, and production of motion pictures, whose career in the industry dated back to the "silents." At the age of seventy-five he became an academician, teaching the art and economics of films to students at Dartmouth College, Stanford University, and the University of Southern California.

He once drafted, with the concurrence of his wife, Lillie, an informal will bequeathing certain spiritual assets to his children and grandchildren. His testament reads, in part:

Without trespassing on the happiness of other children, born or unborn, of any race or clime I, Arthur Mayer, acting on my own behalf and that of my well-loved wife, do make the following bequests to our progeny and to theirs in turn;

—A love of justice. For all the gifts with which we hope to endow you can bring little joy in a world torn by oppression and hatred. The battle against injustice that we have waged all too feebly we entrust to your fresh young hands. In its pursuit you will grow strong and courageous and resourceful. It is the only contest in which success can bring lasting satisfaction, and even defeat has its compensations.

—A love of laughter. For even in the agony of disaster or in the pride of accomplishment, you must remember how to laugh—to laugh kindly at the foibles of others, to laugh with awareness at your own pretensions and petty ambitions, to join in the raucous mirth of the gods at smugness and selfishness seeking to assert themselves for a brief moment on a minute planet swirling through inconceivable space for some incomprehensible purpose.

—A love of your fellows. For it is not enough to fight for man's rights or to laugh at his foibles unless you also hold him dear. Not only the well-washed and the well-bred, the learned and the clever, but the man in the subway and on the farm, the woman in the kitchen and in the office. To sit with him or her in the crossroad store, oblivious of daily duties; while you settle the destiny of the nation, to swap recipes by the fireside, to follow the coon dogs over the hillside, to plan a church social, to match drink for drink and story for story as the night fades into morning—these homely pursuits will shelter you from the sins of cynicism and sophistication and bind you close to the earth from which you sprang. You will learn that knowledge does not come solely from books, or understanding from college courses, and that the natural attributes of all men who are not misled or mistreated are kindness, sincerity, courage and generosity.

—A love of beauty. For without the craving for glowing words and music, color and movement, man would be only a precocious animal who had learnt to stand on two feet, to use two hands to seize food and fashion weapons. And of all life's bounties the love of man for woman and of woman for man—not only of flesh and blood, but of wit and understanding is the most satisfying. But this I do not bother to bequeath to you, convinced as I am that any progeny of Lillie and Arthur, to the most distant generation, will be well aware of and well equipped for its enjoyment.

—A love of nature. For you will not have lived richly unless you have exulted in early spring days, with the faint flush of green on the meadow and buds more felt than seen; in the lushness of summer with the dark shade of the woods along the foaming brown brook where big speckled trout are lurking under well-worn rock; in the crescendo of autumn with the hillsides a blaze of garnet oak and golden birch and russet maple; in the peace of winter with the high snow piled crisp against the old red barn of Mt. Ivy and the big logs aflame and roaring up the fireplace.

—A love of perfection. My final bequest, and I counsel you to value it highly, is to be satisfied with only the best, to hold others, and above all yourselves, to the highest standard of performance. To aim to do at least one thing—whether it be to play the fiddle or dance to it, to plan gracious homes or to defend with eloquence the homes of others, to cure your fellows or to entertain them—with superlative skill. For in the practice and the enhancement of that skill, your self-confidence and your self-mastery will mount, and whatever the vicissitudes and disappointments of life, you will build for yourselves an inexhaustible treasure.

## Living with Style

Style isn't a biblical word, but it's become important in modern communications. We hear frequently about life-styles. And, if you want to say something extravagant about someone—just say she or he has "style."

What that word appears to mean is the ability to be both different and comfortable at the same time.

It describes people not afraid to be themselves, people who are willing, as Henry Thoreau put it, to follow a drumbeat only they are able to hear.

Living *in* style can also mean going first-class. Style, though, isn't primarily about money.

In writing, a person must honor her or his own style.

To *live* with style must also mean to live believing that I am a one-of-a-kind creation, that no one else in the world can offer precisely what I have to offer.

I have my own patented humanity to celebrate. God does not call me to be a carbon copy of someone else.

Charles McCabe of the *San Francisco Chronicle*

says, "Style is the almost necessary by-product of a knowledge of the heart."

In a moving eulogy, a man who had died after a long battle with cancer was described by his son by this sentence, "He died as he lived: with grace, courage, and style."

*my own patented
humanity to celebrate*

# Time

---

*Make the best possible use of your time.* [Colossians 4:5 PHILLIPS]

I have only one thing to do.
   Life's single holy assignment—Luke 10:41-2

I have as much time as anyone.
   All the time in the world—Philippians 4:19

I will set aside moments to be alone.
   Time to be quiet—Matthew 14:23

I will welcome God to my subconscious.
   Clearing the back room—2 Corinthians 5:17

I plan for the future by enjoying today.
   Looking ahead and living now—Luke 14:28-30;
   Matthew 6:34

I do not attempt to do it all.
   No!—Luke 5:15-16

I will make friends with divine interruptions.
   Opportunity in each intrusion—Matthew 9:19-22

I will be courteous of others' time.
   Their time is God's time, too—Luke 6:31

I will live by the secrets of Christian joy.
   The efficiency of gladness—John 15:11

All my time belongs to God.
   The sacrament of every second—
   1 Corinthians 10:31

CHARLIE SHEDD

Philip Bailey wrote: "We live in deeds, not years; in thoughts, not breaths; in feelings, not in figures on a dial. We should count time by heart-throbs."

The question is not, Do I have time? but, Am I awake to myself, to the world, and God? If daily we live but four feet from death, we live an equally short distance from life.

To live is to be neither so tied to the past nor so overpowered by thoughts of the "not yet" that we do not recognize how good it is where we are.

We spend weeks preparing for Christmas. Christmas, though, is drab compared to the fun of getting ready.

*All* life is preparation. That's where the gladness is. The fun of living is journey.

Pick the flowers as you go. Keep your eyes open to wonder. To be alive is to see God in every bush, Christ in every face, the holy in every common thing.

## Good-bye Forever

A boy who lives with a widowed mother is packing his suitcase and preparing to leave for college the next day. It is late afternoon, and the sky is beginning to grow dark.

He is anxious to soften the pain of separation, and he tries to assure his mother that his leaving will be for a limited time. But the mother is wise to the ways of the world. She knows that this farewell has a special quality to it:

It is, in fact, good-bye forever.

'Twill only be for a year, Mother, that I must leave. And the scholarship—it will help me learn so much. And I will learn; I will pass all the examinations. Then, after one year, I will return to you. Wait for me.

Good-bye, my son; good-bye forever. And thank you for the love that will take the scarlet wounds of life's new loneliness, and fill them with the oil of knowing this is the price of a man.

## The Hidden Person of the Heart

Let not yours be the outward adorning with braiding of hair, decoration of gold, and wearing of fine clothing, but let it be the hidden person of the heart with the imperishable jewel of a gentle and quiet spirit, which in God's sight is very precious.

First Letter of Peter 3:3, 4
Revised Standard Version

Antoine de Saint Exupéry lived during the first half of this century and died at age forty-eight. He wrote beautiful things—thoughts and insights that grew out of flying alone high above the earth, coming to appreciate life from a God's-eye point of view. His trilogy of words—*Wind, Sand & Stars* is a heavenly, haunting tune that won't be stilled.

Wind.

Invisible, yet so real. Like the gigantic suction that is created over the wing surfaces of aircraft enabling them to fly, or the force filling a great canvas sail.

Lifting, driving.

How God works in our lives is sometimes difficult to discern. Sometimes winds have hurricane force and are accompanied by storm. Other times our lives seem becalmed—nothing appears to be happening. But then a breeze—and suddenly the timbers creak, the bow-wave appears in front and a vanilla milk-shake wake behind, and we are on our way to some new ports of call.

There's also sand in our shoes. Our sexual lives, our pocketbooks, and politics, our attempts to hammer out human justice, our life in families or as single persons are all intertwined with our interest in prayer and discussions of heaven.

Sand makes us think of castles on the beach.

We build moats and towers and roads— invent worlds of fantasy.

But then the sun falls low in the western sky. The air cools and it's time to go home, so we gather up the beach mats and umbrellas, unread paperbacks, and thermos bottles, and head home, leaving those worlds to be washed away by another tide.

Our greatest happiness comes from building, in the dreaming that takes place, on through the thrill of creating and achievement, in the laughter we share, the flow of the sand through our fingers, the wonder of feeling alive and involved with the universe.

It is not what we leave to later generations that counts. They will have their own fun, make their own sacrifices. The question is not *what* we built, but *how* we did it, what happened to us while construction was underway. Did we encounter God in the midst of all that? Did we "find ourselves"?

And stars.

Stars have always suggested eternity. Because they shine upon us from far-off distances (the light of Riegel takes 500 years at 186,272 m.p.s. to reach us) they stay out of reach and seem to outlast both new and collapsing civilizations. They sing their own aria about permanency and God.

Actually, stars are born, live, and die just like we do, but their span is so much longer we find it hard to take such sequences into account. To us they are as near to foreverness as we can know.

It was a star that led the way to the stable where Jesus was born, and when in the Revelation of John, Jesus is called The Bright and Morning Star, we know there is another kind of guidance God gives to keep us from getting lost.

## Heaven Can Wait, But Can Marriage?

$N$ot everyone is heavily in love when graduation comes, but some are. This short set of lines is for those who are.

Mostly for them, but all may read.

We can love without being "in love," and, in the long run that may be the best kind of loving there is, because love at its finest is not possessive. It does not own another. And it doesn't love for its own selfish sake.

Romantic love may seem to have you in its own strong and present grip; your every thought and action may seem to be saturated by images of someone who has become superspecial in your life. You may find it hard in such a situation to separate those untamable emotions from all your other graduation feelings or to imagine how anything else could possibly be as important as the hope that someday you two might marry.

Marriage is a *process*, not a one-time event. It calls for a lot of grace and endurance. It offers much in the way of fulfilment, but it also asks a lot. It creates fresh boundaries in your life; and that can be both good and, at times, frustrating.

Don't rush marriage. Don't underrate it; but don't overrate it either. You will go on being *you* whether you are single, married, divorced, or widowed.

*You*—as long as you live, and, if the resurrection teachings are valid, even beyond that. This may be one of the most important realities to keep in mind.

Deferring marriage doesn't mean that you have to defer loving. It does mean sacrifice, but it also permits more time to plan, more time to enjoy the unique delights of young singleness, and more time to lay the foundations of a sacred relationship that will stand the test of years.

Marriage is good, but it isn't automatic paradise. Remember, God has made all things beautiful *in their own time.*

*Marriage*
*is a process . . .*

# A Cry Came Ringing Down

The late archaeologist Loren Eiseley, whose books state so much about the history of man and the universe and the spiritual mystique that links us with the stars, describes an experience he once had with a small male hawk he had captured for purposes of scientific study.

He found two birds in an abandoned mountain cabin but was disappointed because he was not able to keep the pair to study; the female got away. He put the male hawk in a small box for the night. The next morning he brought the box out onto the grass with the idea of making a cage. He looked up into the deep blue of the sky to see if there was any sign of the other little hawk, but she had evidently gone for good.

Eiseley describes what happened next:

Secretively, I looked again all around the camp and up and down and opened the box. I got him right out in my hand with his wings folded properly and I was careful not to startle him. He lay limp in my grasp and I could feel his heart pound under the feathers but he only looked beyond me and up.

I saw him look that last look away beyond me into a sky so full of light that I could not follow his gaze.

The little breeze flowed over me again, and nearby a mountain aspen shook all its tiny leaves. I suppose I must have had an idea then of what I was going to do, but I never let it come up into consciousness. I just reached over and laid the hawk on the grass.

He lay there a long minute without hope, unmoving, his eyes still fixed on that blue vault above him. It must have been that he was already so far away in heart that he never felt the release of my hand. He never even stood. He just lay with his breast against the grass.

In the next second after that long minute he was gone. Like a flicker of light, he had vanished with my eyes full on him, but without actually seeing even a premonitory wing beat. He was gone straight into that towering emptiness of light and crystal that my eyes could scarcely bear to penetrate. For another long moment there was silence. I could not see him. The light was too intense. Then from far up somewhere a cry came ringing down.

I was young then and had seen little of the world, but when I heard that cry my heart turned over. It was not the cry of the hawk I had captured; for, by shifting my position against the sun, I was now seeing further up. Straight out of the sun's eye, where she must have been soaring restlessly above us for untold hours, hurtled his mate. And from far up, ringing from peak to peak of the summits over us, came a cry of such unutterable and ecstatic joy that it sounds down across the years and tingles among the cups on my quiet breakfast table.

—from *The Immense Journey* by Loren Eiseley
© 1955. Used by permission of Random House, Inc.

# I See the Beginning of Eloquence

My son brought home an English theme one day from Palisades High School.

As a marginal notation beside one of his better paragraphs, his teacher had written, "I see the beginning of eloquence."

This is what we all want others to see as we pass by.

## Not All *Wings Are Made of Tapered Feathers*

Roots have a way of turning into wings when the issue of who we are is resolved in favor of an ability to believe in ourselves because we believe God has a reason for our being here and work for us to do.

Angels are often pictured as flying about with white, scalloped wings. But not all wings are made of tapered feathers.

Dreams are wings.

Imagination, too.

And don't leave out courage.

We also share the eagle life by slowly learning to pray:

Prayer always creates a new situation.

We also learn to claim our own personalized pair of wings when we let ourselves become embraced within some community of believers that helps to lift us out of our solitariness or loneliness, freeing us from limitations that hold us back when we insist on trying to make it alone. Or when we won't allow ourselves to be forgiven, loved, and made whole by those who share this same fallible, fabulous journey with us—plodding along through what Frederick Buechner called the "fragrant muck."

We enjoy the lift of those wings, then we learn to hope. Hoping enables us to soar and see distances.

Air Force pilot Colonel John Stavast spent five and a half years in a North Vietnamese prison camp, seemingly doomed.

During his long imprisonment, the members of his church regularly prayed for him.

One Friday morning the word came. Nothing had been heard, even indirectly, for over four years. Then suddenly, a few words that seemed not very newsworthy, yet said everything everyone wanted to hear—John Stavast was alive!

Eventually the day arrived when he returned to the United States. Then one day, thinner, but tall, handsome, and smiling he walked down the aisle of the sanctuary as the congregation burst into applause.

John and his wife Shirley live in Texas now, but gave a handsome thanksgiving remembrance to the congregation—a bronze eagle— with some words from the prophet Isaiah inscribed on its base:

Those who wait upon the Lord shall renew their strength . . . they shall mount up with wings as eagles; they shall run and not be weary; they shall walk and not faint.

"High Flight" is the soliloquy of another young serviceman caught up in the mystique of flying a plane, alone, miles above the Earth.

O, I have slipped the surly bonds of earth.
And danced the skies on laughter-silvered wings.
Sunward I've climbed, and joined the tumbling mirth
Of sun-split clouds—
And done a hundred things you have not dreamed of—
Wheeled and soared and swung, high in the sunlit silence.
Hov'ring there I've chased the shouting wind along,
And flung my eager craft through footless halls of Air. Up, up the long, delirious burning blue I've Topped the wind-swept heights with easy grace and
While, with silent lifting mind I've trod the high, Untrespassed sanctity of space . . . Put out my hand,
And touched the face of God.

"You gave me two things," wrote this young woman graduate, fresh from her own mortarboard ceremony: "the two best things any parents can give their children. You gave me roots and wings."

They are, to be sure, two gifts, beyond all price. Faith to root us in the love of God, wings to bear us up and speed us out into our own futures unafraid.

# Why Pray?

Prayer always creates a new situation.

That's better than saying prayer changes things.

Prayer is not magical—it may not evoke a sudden change—because it does not involve the short-circuiting of God's ordered universe. We cannot draw our own little blue circles around what prayer will achieve and what it won't. God doesn't take orders from us. But we distort prayer as a means of grace if we fail to understand that God's principal gift to us in prayer is the gift of the splendid Spirit.

Prayer to a god who responds to us whimsically would be a spirit of slavery, leading us back into a life of fear. It would be primitive groveling before some monstrous, arms-folded deity!

God, heal my leg. God, find me a job. Help me stop drinking.

We have all prayed prayers that belong in that category, and we will pray more of them before our lives are over. Sometimes life closes in upon us so ruthlessly we cry these emergency cries, and we're not about to stop and ask whether they are legitimate or not.

But prayer, understood at its best—prayer in the spirit of Christ—is prayer *for* His Spirit. Prayer, regardless of what comes, or doesn't come, enables us to fashion the facts into a new part of an unfolding will. It is a prayer to love, to trust; sometimes, to wait.

What is the fresh situation prayer creates? If God doesn't rush in to take our side, do our bidding, or pluck us out of the path of danger, what difference does praying make? Partly this: Prayer renews our humanity. It changes how we feel about ourselves so that we function differently—with less anger, less tension, less concern for what is going to happen to us, and more concern about others.

# Cheerleading and Limits

The young woman who wrote about roots and wings would also, I suspect, find to her liking the dad who, looking at the parent-child relationship from the other end, said that what he had tried to be to his children was a cheerleader and a setter of limits.

We all need people in our lives who keep telling us that we're great and that we can do it—a cheering section. And, though we may kick and complain and protest at the time, if we're this side of eighteen or twenty-one, we also half secretly appreciate parents who provide us with a framework of limits in which to explore our freedom and emerge into our own worlds of independence and identity.

Thanks, Pop.

Thanks, Mom.

Thanks for helping me recognize and enjoy some victories along the way. And thanks for occasionally saying no.

# A Prescription for Peace

Strike a balance between work and play, between seriousness and laughter. Go to church regularly. Also to the ballgame.

Stick with the truth even if it makes you look or feel bad. Falsehoods are wandering ghosts.

Forgive your enemies as part of the price you pay for the privilege of being forgiven.

Realize that you are sometimes "a pain in the neck" yourself.

Walk. Get lots of air and sunshine. Occasionally some rain or snow in your face, some dirt on your hands.

Talk your troubles over with someone you trust. Your dreams, too.

Don't underestimate the ability of God to straighten out a situation, even when you can't. Give him a little time.

Discriminate among your fears. Learn to tell which ones are useful, which ones destructive.

Remember that the ultimate death rate is still 100%. You would be getting gyped if everyone got to die and you didn't.

When you can't sleep, say: Aha! Here's a chance for a little privacy and creative thinking. All day long I've been too busy to pray; now I can get around to thanking God.

Fall in love with life, with children, older people, sportscars, the theater, music, books, cities, hills, the Bible—everything except money.

## Parents Want to Say "Thank You," Too!

Graduation may provoke thank-you expressions from seniors to their parents: "Gee, you were great through all those years of my growing up." But such thank-yous also run in the opposite direction.

Those of us who are mothers and fathers have our piece to speak as well. We thank you for being our children, for adding such fabulous joy and inexpressible meaning to our own existences.

Sure, you were problems at times. And so were we. But you gave to us what no supermarket can sell and no money can buy . . . you gave us important reasons to live, and you gave us love by letting us love you.

Now we pray for the brave sort of love that will let you go . . . that will free you to live your own lives according to your own dreams . . . that will enable you to become the glorious human creations life is waiting for and which date back to your own conceptions.

We release you. And pardon the tears.

God protect you.

You've given us roots and wings, too.

## Acknowledgments and Thanks

To all whose lives and words have provided inspiration and authenticity to Roots and Wings—especially to Michael F. Mayer for sharing his father's will; to Virginia Satir for the lines beginning, "I want to love . . ." (words which also grace the walls of my study); to John Gillespie Magee's family for "High Flight"; to Charlie Shedd for *Time for All Things* (Nashville: Abingdon Press, 1962, 1980); to Clarence G. Scholl without whose urging and expertise this little book would not have been; and to my own four children whose high school graduations have left a permanent and happy impression upon my life.

*James W. Angell*